DISCOVERING DI

ARMORED DINOSAURS

Jinny Johnson

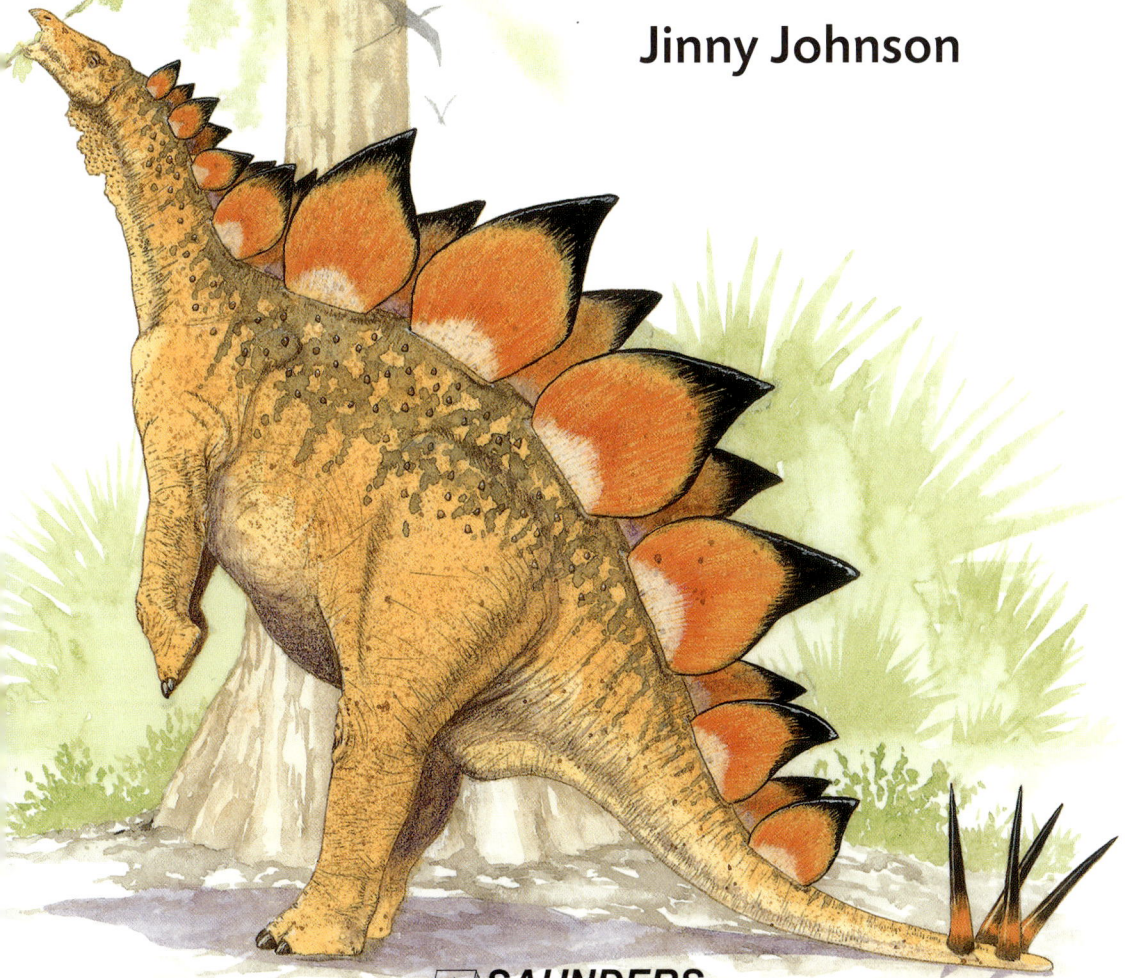

SAUNDERS
BOOK COMPANY

Published by Saunders Book Company
27 Stewart Road, Collingwood, ON Canada L9Y 4M7

Printed in the United States of America, at Corporate
Graphics in North Mankato, Minnesota.

Illustrated by Graham Rosewarne
Designed by Hel James
Edited by Mary-Jane Wilkins

Cataloging-in-Publication Data is available
from the Library of Congress

ISBN 978-1-77092-160-3 (paperback)

Picture credit
Front cover Merlinul/Shutterstock

DAD0511
052013
9 8 7 6 5 4 3 2 1

Contents

Inside a Dinosaur

A dinosaur was a kind of reptile that lived millions of years ago. We know about dinosaurs because many of their bones and teeth have been found.

Some dinosaurs had their own armor. Triceratops and other horned dinosaurs had bony frills and huge horns. Nodosaurs and ankylosaurs were covered in pieces of bone, and stegosaurs had bony plates along their backs.

This is what a Triceratops looked like inside.

There weren't any people on Earth when dinosaurs were alive. The picture gives you an idea of how big each dinosaur was compared with a seven-year-old child.

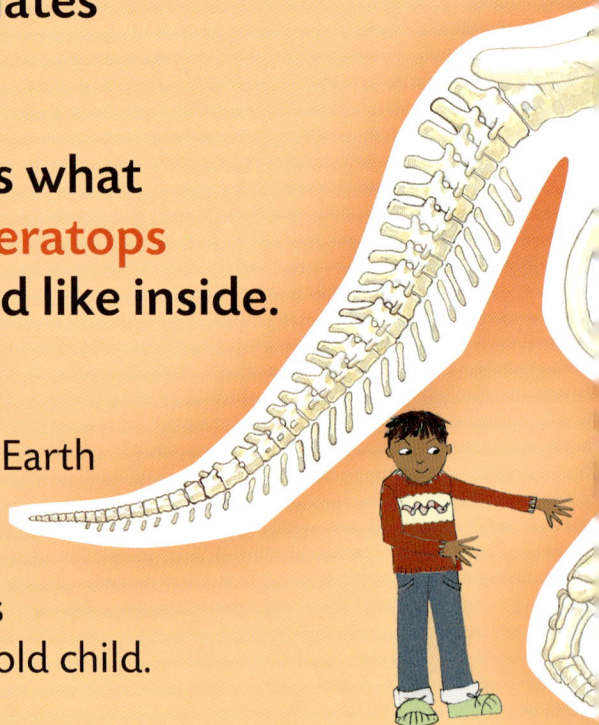

Scientists divide the time when dinosaurs lived into three periods: the Triassic, Jurassic, and Cretaceous. At the beginning of the Triassic period, all the world's land was joined. The land gradually split up into smaller areas to make the world we know today.

Triassic Period: 250–00 million years ago
Jurassic Period: 200–145 million years ago
Cretaceous Period: 145–65 million years ago

Neck frill: solid bone, heavy and strong

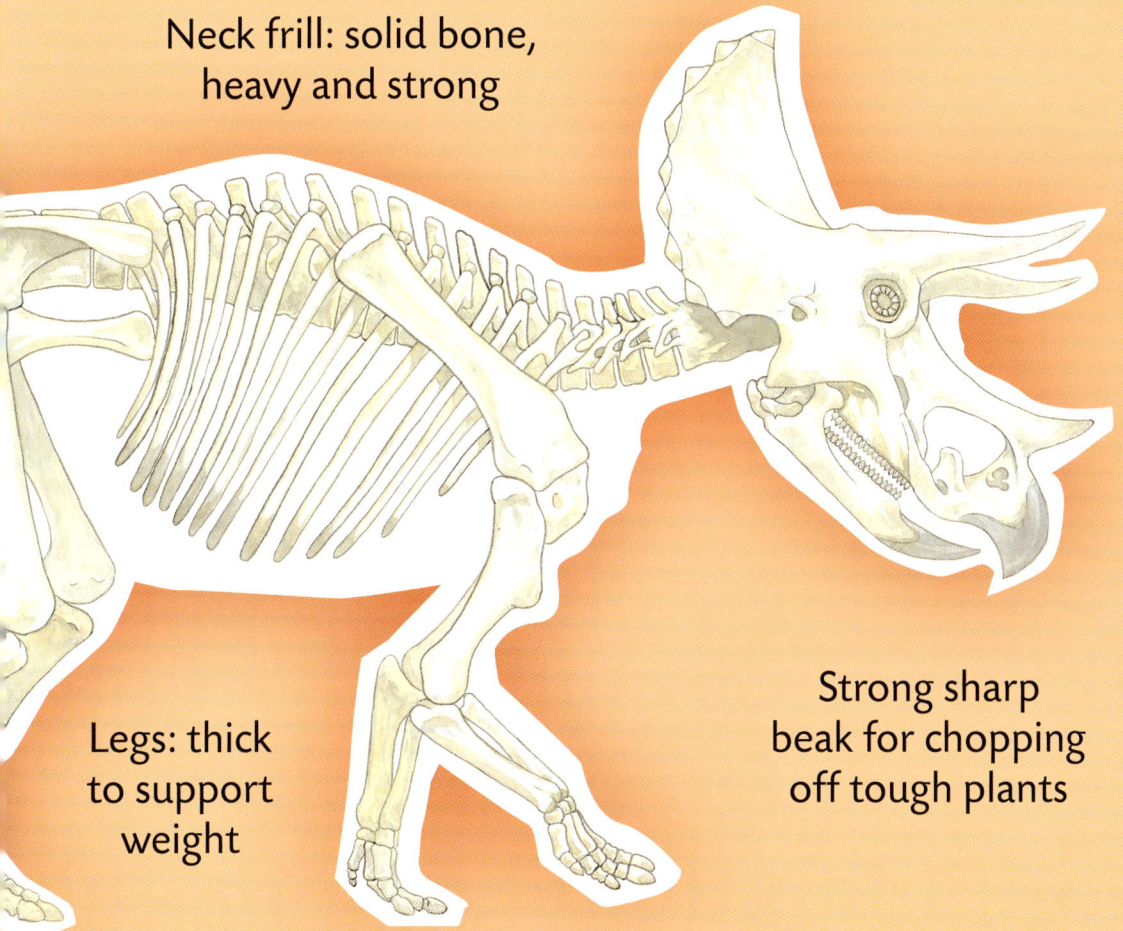

Legs: thick to support weight

Strong sharp beak for chopping off tough plants

Triceratops

Imagine a creature twice the size of a rhinoceros, with an **enormous** head. That was **Triceratops**.

It had three sharp horns and a large **bony frill** at the back of its neck. **Triceratops** was strong enough to fight off the fiercest of attackers —even Tyrannosaurus!

Try saying this
dinosaur's name:
Tri-serra-tops

DINO FACTS
ABOUT 29 FEET
(9 M) LONG
LIVED 67–65 MILLION
YEARS AGO

Short-frilled Dinosaurs

There were other kinds of horned dinosaurs. Some had short neck frills. Others had *l o n g e r* ones.

Centrosaurus and **Pachyrhinosaurus** had short neck frills.

Try saying this dinosaur's name: Cen-tro-sore-us

Their horns and spikes made them look very fierce.

Try saying this dinosaur's name: Pack-ee-rine-o-sore-us

Long-frilled Dinosaurs

These **horned dinosaurs** had very l o n g neck **frills** that made them hard to **attack**.

Try saying this dinosaur's name:
Tor-o-sore-us

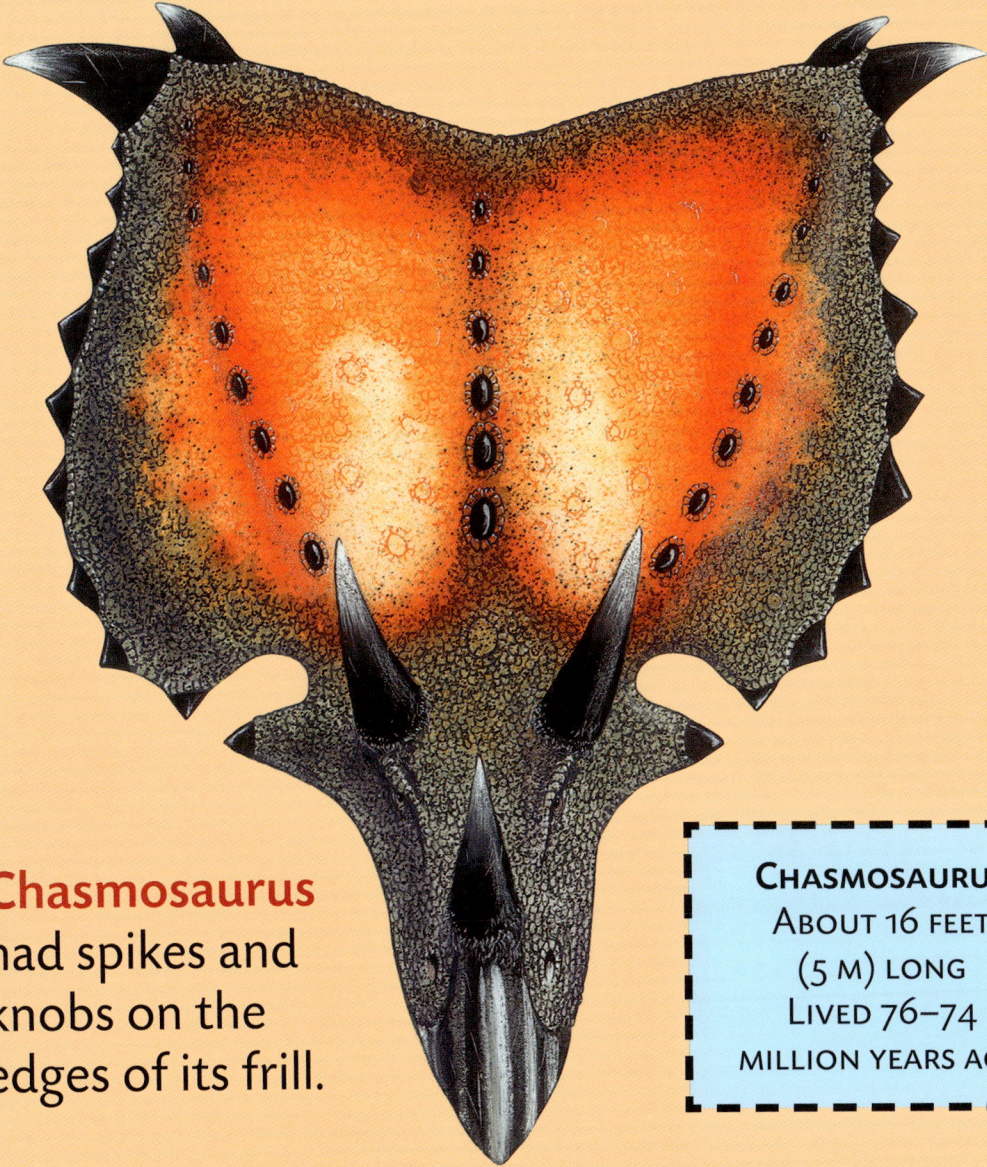

Chasmosaurus had spikes and knobs on the edges of its frill.

CHASMOSAURUS
ABOUT 16 FEET
(5 M) LONG
LIVED 76–74
MILLION YEARS AGO

Try saying this dinosaur's name:
Kas-mo-sore-us

Nodosaurs

These dinosaurs were like **walking tanks**. They had flat pieces of bone set into their skin and big sharp spikes sticking out of their sides.

Sauropelta was one of the largest and was heavier than a rhinoceros. **Panoplosaurus** had pieces of bone on its head for extra protection.

Try saying this dinosaur's name: Sore-o-pelt-ah

**Try saying this
dinosaur's name:
Pan-o-ploh-sore-us**

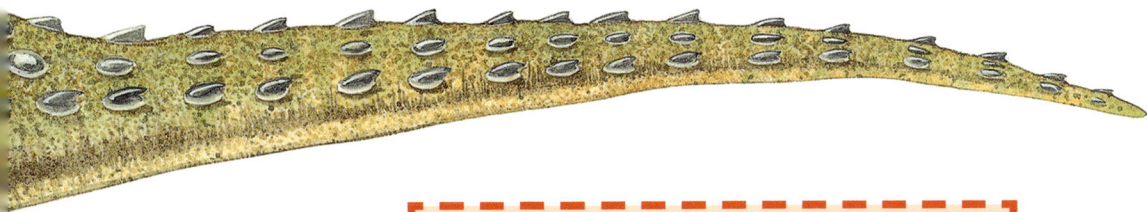

SAUROPELTA
ABOUT 21 FEET (6.5 M) LONG
LIVED 121–94 MILLION YEARS AGO

Ankylosaurs

These **huge** dinosaurs had even more armor than nodosaurs. Their eyelids had pieces of bone that came down over their eyes like shutters.

Try saying this dinosaur's name: Sy-chan-ee-a

SAICHANIA
ABOUT 21 FEET (6.5 M) LONG
LIVED 80 MILLION YEARS AGO

Ankylosaurs had a heavy club of bone at the end of their tails. They could swing this against an attacker's legs and break them.

Try saying this dinosaur's name:
You-o-plo-kef-a-lus

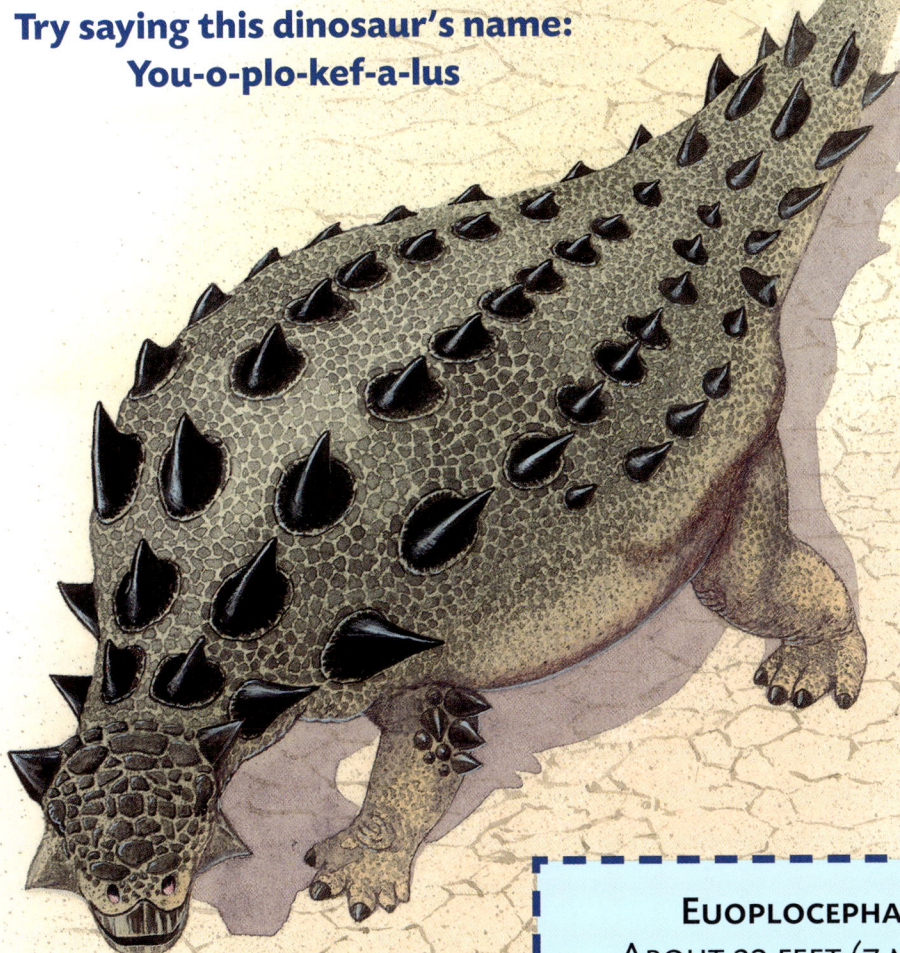

Boneheaded Dinosaurs

These dinosaurs had dome-shaped skulls with a thick lump of bone in the front.

Males probably fought fierce battles in the breeding season. Their **extra-thick** skulls protected them when they crashed into one another.

> **STEGOCERAS**
> UP TO 8 FEET (2.5 M) LONG
> LIVED 76–74 MILLION YEARS AGO

**Try saying this dinosaur's name:
Steg-os-er-as**

Pachycephalosaurus was the biggest boneheaded dinosaur. The dome on its head grew thicker as the dinosaur got older.

PACHYCEPHALOSAURUS
ABOUT 26 FEET (8 M) LONG
LIVED 76–65 MILLION YEARS AGO

**Try saying this dinosaur's name:
Pack-ee-kef-al-o-sore-us**

Stegosaurs

These dinosaurs had large, triangular bony plates along their back. The plates were probably covered with skin.

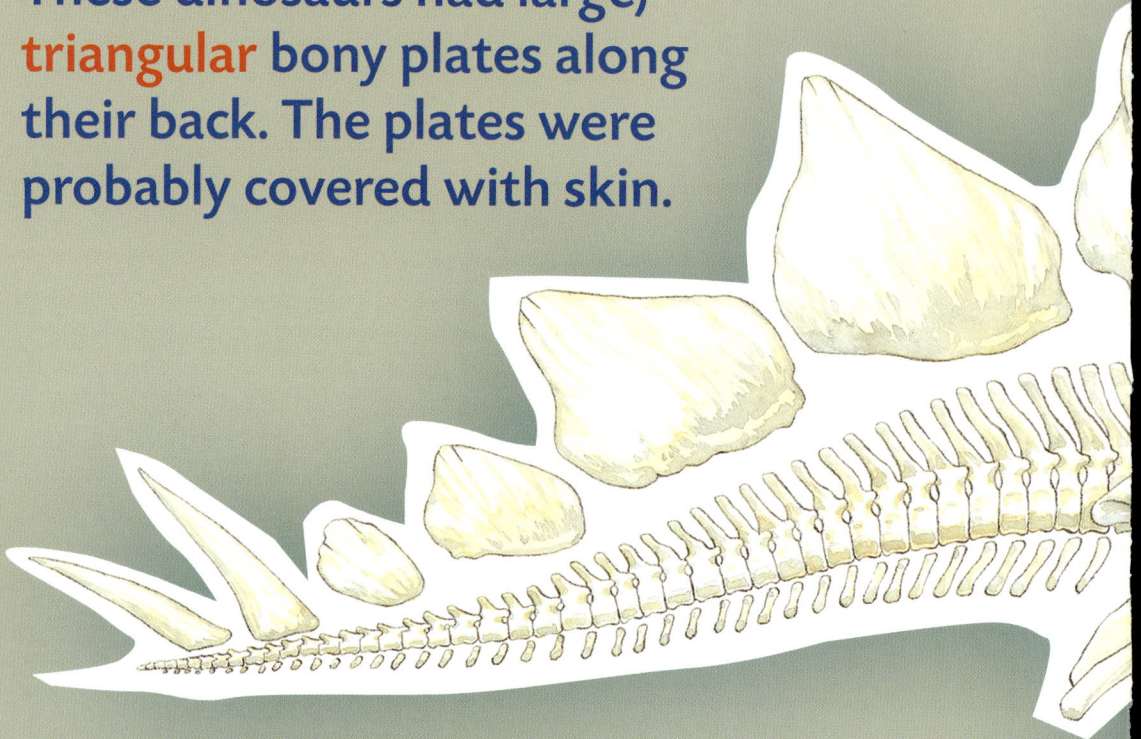

Stegosaurus was the largest stegosaur. Its body was bigger than an elephant's, but its head was tiny.

Heavy leg bones to support weight

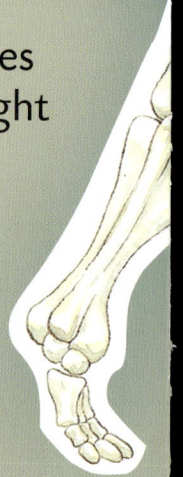

Stegosaurus's back legs were longer than its front legs. This made its body *slope down* so its mouth was nearer the ground when it was feeding.

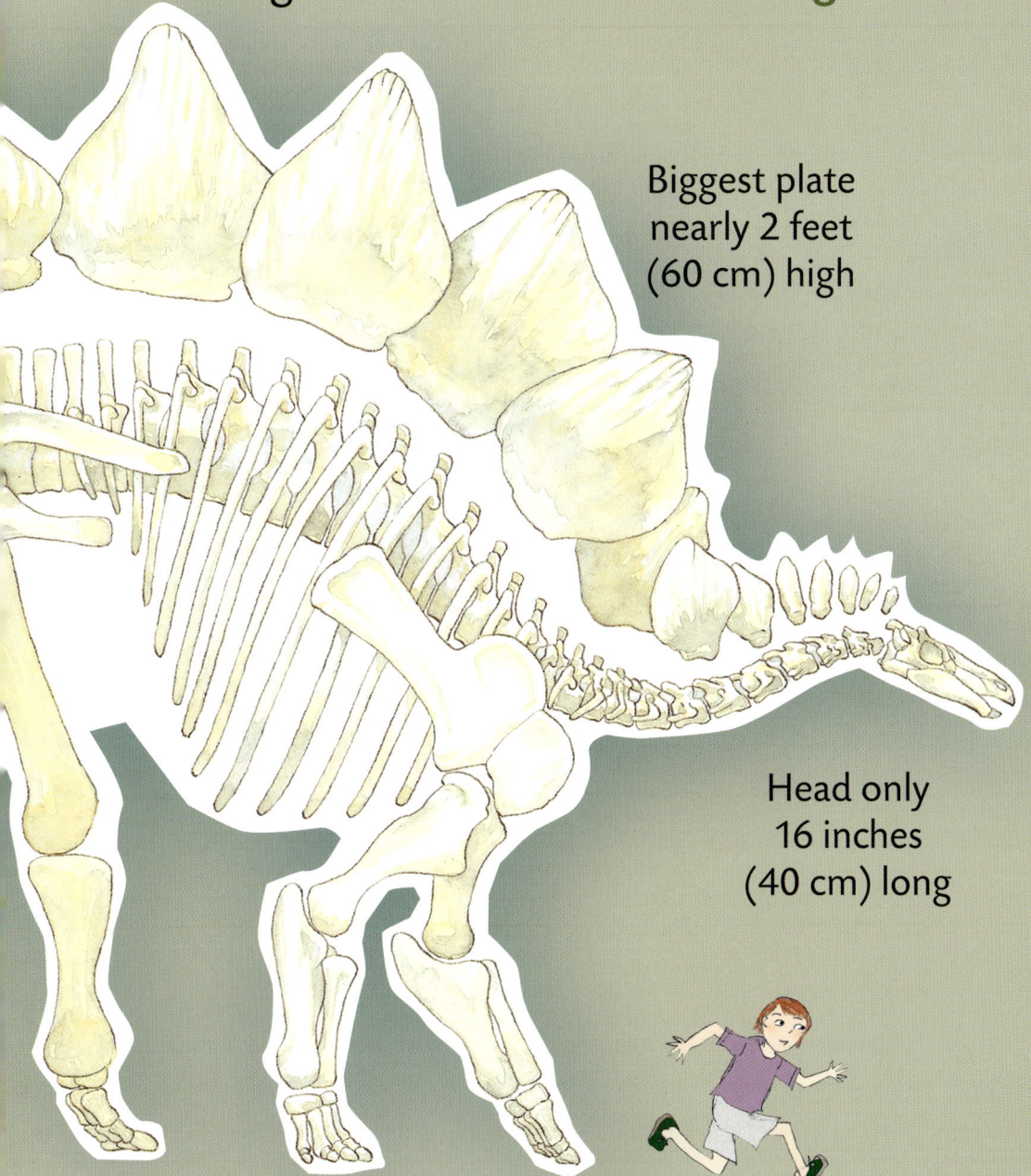

Biggest plate nearly 2 feet (60 cm) high

Head only 16 inches (40 cm) long

Stegosaurus in Action

Stegosaurus gobbled up tough leaves with the **sharp toothless beak** at the front of its mouth. It probably spent most of the day feeding, just like *plant-eating* animals today.

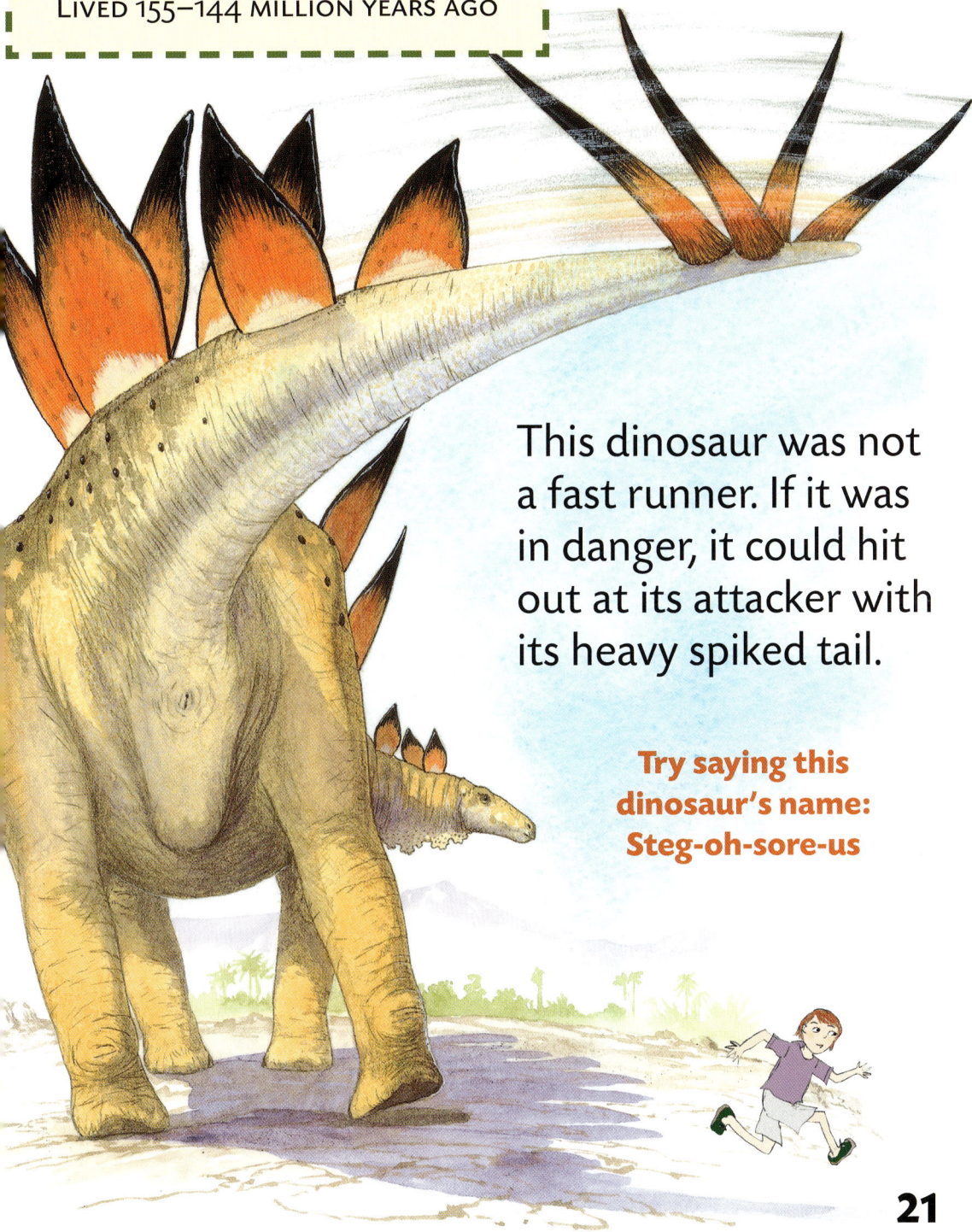

This dinosaur was not a fast runner. If it was in danger, it could hit out at its attacker with its heavy spiked tail.

Try saying this dinosaur's name: Steg-oh-sore-us

Spiky Stegosaurs

Bony plates may have helped protect a stegosaur from predators. Or they may have helped it warm up or cool down.

When a stegosaur was cold it turned towards the sun. The heat of the sun warmed the blood as it passed through the skin on the bony plates.

Try saying this dinosaur's name:
Lex-o-vee-sore-us

When the dinosaur felt too hot it faced the *wind*, which cooled the bony plates and the dinosaur's blood.

Try saying this dinosaur's name:
Too-yang-o-sore-us

TUOJIANGOSAURUS
UP TO 23 FEET (7 M) LONG
LIVED 157–154 MILLION YEARS AGO

Words to Remember

neck frill
The sheet of bone at the back of a horned dinosaur's head.

predator
An animal that hunts and kills other animals.

reptile
An animal with a backbone and a scaly body. Dinosaurs were reptiles. Today's reptiles include lizards, snakes, and crocodiles.

Tyrannosaurus
A large meat-eating dinosaur, which attacked plant-eating dinosaurs.

Index